Skim, Scan, Scroll

A quick guide to web writing

Jyotsna Atre

UNICORN BOOKS

Publishers
UNICORN BOOKS
J-3/16, Daryaganj, New Delhi-110002
☎ 23276539, 23272783, 23272784 • *Fax:* 011-23260518
E-mail: unicornbooks@vsnl.com
Website: www.unicornbooks.in • www.kidscorner.in

Distributors
Pustak Mahal®, Delhi

London Office
51, Severn Crescents, Slough, Berkshire, SL 38 UU, England
E-mail: pustakmahaluk@pustakmahal.com

Sales Centre
10-B, Netaji Subhash Marg, Daryaganj, New Delhi-110002
☐ 23268292, 23268293, 23279900 • *Fax:* 011-23280567

Branch Offices
Bangalore: ☐ 22234025
E-mail: pmblr@sancharnet.in • pustak@sancharnet.in
Mumbai: ☐ 22010941
E-mail: rapidex@bom5.vsnl.net.in
Patna: ☐ 3094193 • *Telefax:* 0612-2302719
E-mail: rapidexptn@rediffmail.com
Hyderabad: *Telefax:* 040-24737290
E-mail: pustakmahalhyd@yahoo.co.in

ISBN :978-81-7806-145-0

Edition : February 2008

Printed at : Param Offsetters, Okhla, New Delhi-110020

Contents

Introduction

The title of this book pretty much tells you what you can expect to read between the covers. No guessing there. And considering that you are still holding the book, I presume that you are interested in uploading a piece of prose on *the Web*. There could be a thousand different reasons why. Maybe you want to put together content that informs your website visitors of your business. Perhaps you are looking to make your blog more interesting, and up your reader-base. Or, you already write in magazines and newspapers, and want to know what goes into writing for the web.

Good start. Looking back, when I first turned my attention to the web in the 1990s, there weren't many resources I could tap to know about the medium, its audience or how to hold their attention. Amazon was a nascent idea, they didn't ship their books to India, and in any case, struggling writers didn't possess credit cards to pay for them! So I decided that the neighbourhood bookstores would be the best bet to gear my writing for the web. Unfortunately, many hours of browsing through book-lined shelves could not return any relevant results. All I found were step-by-step software guides for web designers, html handbooks for programmers, and exhaustive manuals for webmasters. But, no one was telling me how to write the *text* that the web pages were programmed and designed to show!

I am not sure this situation has changed much. A few months ago, when I raided the bookstores to look for information on how web writing techniques have evolved over the years, I drew a blank yet again. Even a decade and a half later, it seems that text is an afterthought when it comes to putting up a website. That was when I decided to bridge the gap.

As a writer, I firmly believe that content is king. In fact, biased as I am, I will go so far to say that the written word is why the web exists! No scripting language or flashy graphics are going to retain your visitors, if they do not find the information (read text!) that they can use. And although the Internet is a visual medium, quite like the television, it is far more closely related to the print medium where the written word captivates the audience. That tells us why good writing is the key element of a good website.

It's Different!

What is so different about writing for the web, you might want to ask. After all, almost all of us have done some kind of writing. And how different can writing school essays, or business letters, or newspaper articles, or a journal be from writing for a website? Doesn't writing involve...well...just writing? Yes and no.

Writing is an art that is inborn. Take the school essay for instance. As we struggle to string our ideas on a piece of paper and hope for a passable six on ten, in our hearts of hearts, we know that the world is divided into two categories of people—those that can write and those that cannot. And if you belong to the first category, you know that there is more to your writing than just content. Form is just as important. Ask any talented writer and they will tell you that in this era of mass media, we need to be aware of the demands of the medium that we are writing for, be it the print, the screen or the web.

Ironically, although both print and web media involve publishing the written word for reading unlike the television, writing for the web is quite, quite different from writing for print. That's because just like the print medium, the World Wide Web too has its share of strengths and weaknesses.

Where's the Time?

The biggest weakness of the virtual medium is that its readers just don't have the time. No one is logging into their accounts to read through a thousand words of skilfully crafted introduction (the way I am doing right now) and a body of argument that takes up 30-odd pages, before they finally get to read the climax of your story.

Try this typical 'print' method of writing on the web, and chances are that your reader will have clicked away to another web page or worse, jumped away to another website before you can even say your opening lines. Imagine what that means for the service or the product that you are writing for. Marketing gurus would compare it to committing hara-kiri! After all, the raison d'être of your (or your client's) website is to get the visitors to read as much as they possibly can, so that they know all that they possibly can, as quickly as they possibly can.

Quite clearly, you are playing by a different set of rules here, and facing a difficult audience.

Where's the Space?

That's right. Unlike the print medium, where the reader gets a book, magazine, newspaper, brochure, or a leaflet that holds all the information together, the web offers you a single screen to work with. And if you thought that all those 1280 x 768 pixels belonged to you...think again! Logos, links, graphics, opinion polls, forms, copyright announcements...there are a thousand things in there jostling for space. And then there's your text, in muted shades of grey that must make the point right here right now, else click goes your reader!

That means, when a visitor reaches your web page, you must be able to quickly give them the relevant information and persuade them to click on the 'Next' button, so you can talk to them some more. And repeat this cycle until they have browsed through your entire website, without getting bored or restless.

Where's the Motivation?

Often, when a reader picks up a product from the print medium, they are loyal readers of the newspaper or magazine. Or they have heard about a certain author or a book and want to read the story. There's a reason why they buy the product. But on the web, visitors usually reach your website accidentally—through search engines, through affiliate programs, or through links that they randomly find and *think* can yield information. Very rarely will anyone remember a URL and type it in the address bar to access your website.

Since they don't actively seek you out, the onus to keep them interested and asking for more is on you. Give them specific information that they can use, and they will stay. But upload some profound blah, and no one will have the time or the inclination to read on.

Reader Rules

"...79 percent of our test users always scanned any new page they came across; only 16 percent read word-by-word."

— Jakob Nielsen

But, why are web readers such an impatient lot?

1. Because reading text on the monitor strains the eyes, a person will read screen text far more slowly than when reading in print. In fact, on-screen reading can physically tire you after a few hours. So, reading on the computer screen is not a very pleasant experience.
2. Because readers are easily distracted if they don't find the information that they are looking for. And if they can click on a link to reach your website, there's the danger that they can also go somewhere else. After all, another website is just a click away.
3. Because, and most importantly, people don't read web pages word by word like they do on paper. In fact, research shows that people scan web pages, focussing on particular words and sentences.

Surprised? Think back to your own surfing habits, and you will realise that 'skim, scan, scroll' is your own mantra on the web. You hurriedly skim through the content to see if there's anything that might interest you. You scan to see if you want to read the written word at all. At best you quickly scroll the page, and then swiftly click the mouse.

What you are doing is corroborating research findings, which show that only a third of a site's visitors will ever read a whole article. Eight out of ten visitors will go away after scanning the headlines, summaries, and captions. Fortunately, there's a structure to their impatience. Readers will progress by scanning first for the headlines, subheadings, summaries, keywords or phrases and hyperlinks. In that order!

And as a web writer, this is your biggest chance. You can learn to use each of these as tools to effectively keep the visitors glued to your web page and asking for more.

In the pages that follow, we will see just how to do that.

One Size Doesn't Fit All

There are over 30 million active websites on the Internet and hundreds of new ones are going online every day.

These websites can be classified into different types, depending on the purpose that they serve, such as sharing information, providing entertainment, facilitating communication or conducting commercial transactions.

Whatever the category they belong to, no two websites ever want to be the same. Each one exists to create a niche for the service they offer or the product they sell or the entity they publicise.

Use A Different Pitch

As a prolific web writer, you will get a chance to work on a variety of websites. It will certainly get your creative juices flowing, but at the same time, you have to rise to the challenge of writing copy that *'speaks'* differently to your unique audience.

Obviously, you will write in a different way for corporate websites, news websites, sales landing pages, or blogs. The key to effective web writing is that different types of websites demand different types of writing. So, let's take a look at the types of websites that you are likely to write for, and their content needs.

Corporate websites

Corporate websites are very different from the routine corporate presentations with the contact information thrown in. Think of them as an office in the virtual space and you will see why they need to be an effective channel of communications and should aim to deliver quality information and services to their users.

When a firm hires you to write for their website, you are not only providing information to users about the company, its services and products, but also helping to build the corporate brand. Make sure that you talk about the mission, vision, philosophy and the history of the company and provide descriptions of the products/services. Also give out the names of the key management people and make sure that you answer the FAQs.

Personal websites

If the guy of your dreams asks you out for dinner, and you want to shout from your rooftop to let the world know, we can't really blame you. But perhaps, putting it up on your personal website would be a better option.

Personal websites are just that...personal. They could be hosted by families to update other members of their family. Or it might be an individual trying to chronicle life-as-it-happens. You could even choose to convert this space into your virtual diary to share your feelings, observations, opinions, experiences and events in your personal life such as the birth of a baby or an upcoming wedding with family, friends and virtually anyone who finds it interesting, in near real-time.

Unfortunately, personal websites remain outside the mainstream web although some of them do have interesting little stories. This is because, more often than not, their owners don't understand the rules of dramatic plot construction. So, if you plan to get your very own 10 MB of space on GeoCities or Yahoo or the countless other free website hosting services, be sure that your story has drama and a twist in the tale that is sensitive, funny, or enthralling. Even your friends will love it.

Professionals can use personal websites as their online résumé. But don't walk the routine way. Use it to communicate your personality in a casual, conversational manner like in the example below, instead of putting up an uninspiring chronology of your work history!

Flash websites

Flash is a tool that quite literally allows you to make 'flashy' websites. But as a writer, your concern should be about how your text will be displayed, and how much writing space you will get. That's because websites made using Flash are rich in visual content, (such as graphics, animation and video) and almost resemble a television. They are a great way to advertise a product or a service. Since the focus here is on the moving image and the well-designed interface, your job as a writer becomes all the more challenging. You must write copy that packs in the maximum punch with the minimum of words.

Sales pages

Quite often, especially these days, we reach websites that are nothing more than a single, long page with information about a product (usually e-books), interspersed with client testimonials and limited time discount offers.

These sites are called 'landing pages' and are used for promoting online sales. Needless to say, sales pages need you to write promotional copy about the product in a very persuasive, yet conversational tone, almost like a sales letter.

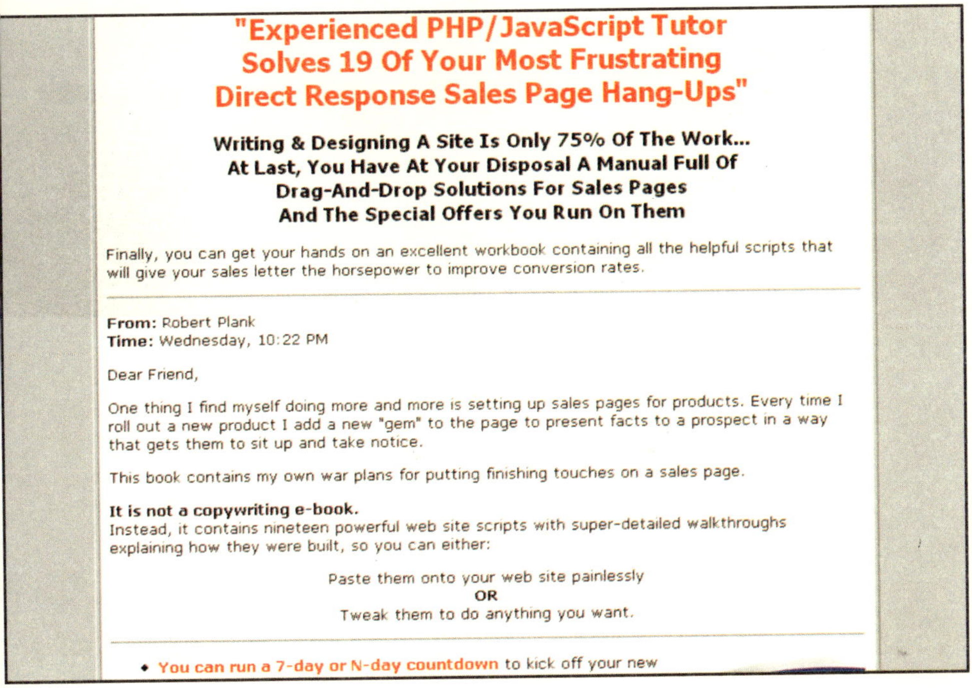

"Experienced PHP/JavaScript Tutor Solves 19 Of Your Most Frustrating Direct Response Sales Page Hang-Ups"

Writing & Designing A Site Is Only 75% Of The Work...
At Last, You Have At Your Disposal A Manual Full Of Drag-And-Drop Solutions For Sales Pages And The Special Offers You Run On Them

Finally, you can get your hands on an excellent workbook containing all the helpful scripts that will give your sales letter the horsepower to improve conversion rates.

From: Robert Plank
Time: Wednesday, 10:22 PM

Dear Friend,

One thing I find myself doing more and more is setting up sales pages for products. Every time I roll out a new product I add a new "gem" to the page to present facts to a prospect in a way that gets them to sit up and take notice.

This book contains my own war plans for putting finishing touches on a sales page.

It is not a copywriting e-book.
Instead, it contains nineteen powerful web site scripts with super-detailed walkthroughs explaining how they were built, so you can either:

Paste them onto your web site painlessly
OR
Tweak them to do anything you want.

- **You can run a 7-day or N-day countdown** to kick off your new

If you are writing one, start with a catchy headline and then follow up with several short briefs about the product (product description, why it is better, what it offers, how you will benefit, etc.) throughout the page. These product briefs are interspersed with 'sign up', 'register' or 'purchase now' offers. After all, the aim of a sales page is to make as many conversions (or get as many clicks as possible!).

Intranets

If the Internet is the network that connects you to the world, the Intranet closes you within a group. Intranets are typically private networks hosted by large companies on their servers and are increasingly becoming important in the business world as a corporate information network. That's because the Intranet has firewalls that prevent users from outside the company group from accessing its contents.

The Intranet is mostly used to promote employee interaction, especially for companies with offices located across the country or around the world.

While it allows workgroups to conference online, more importantly, it is used to store internal document systems, such as procedure manuals, training materials, requisition forms, etc.

Blogs

Short for web logs, here is the online avatar of your good ole' diary!

Blogs are online journals that are updated frequently, sometimes even daily. An update is a short entry or a post to which your readers can respond online. Mostly created by individuals, blogs are a series of articles listed in reverse chronological order. These articles can be the random ramblings of a writer, or incisive, informative commentaries about a cause/event. You can register yourself on these blogs and write your comments about these articles.

Blogs are known for their casual writing and unpredictable subject material. Here are some guiding principles for writing a successful blog.

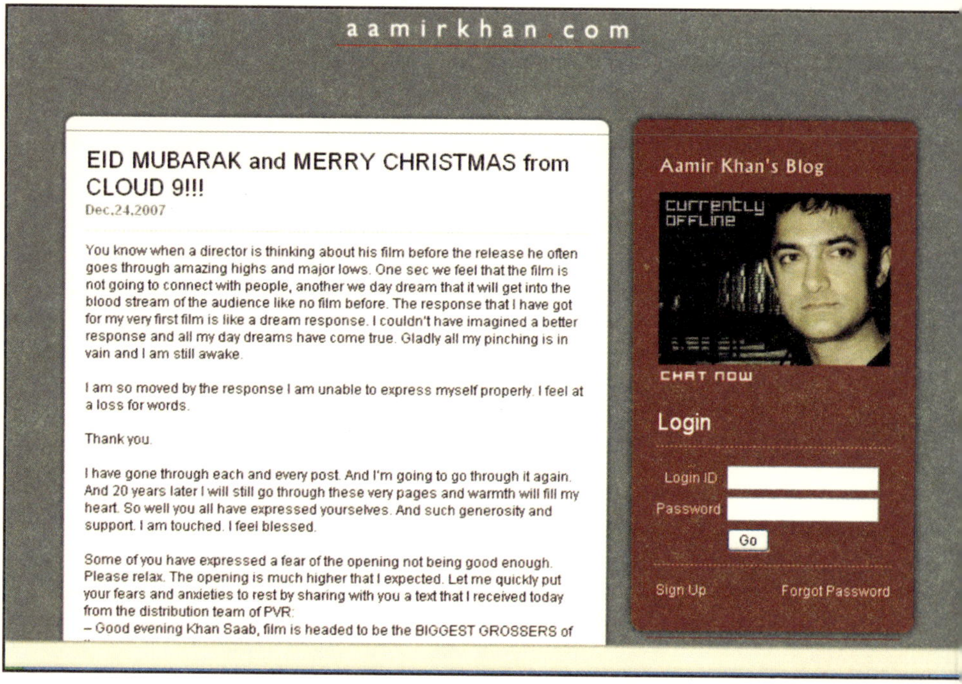

1. Develop a writing style and voice appropriate to your subject material.
2. Post often, even if your posts are short.
3. *Talk* to your readers.
4. Allow your readers to comment on your posts.
5. Cool design or state-of-the-art programming tools cannot replace an interesting, readable post.

E-commerce websites

Many retailers prefer e-commerce websites to 'brick and mortar' sales points. These websites allow you to buy something online and pay for it online as well. Amazon.com is a very good and a very successful example of an e-commerce website. As a writer, your role, however, may be limited to writing product reviews to help the visitor make a purchasing decision.

Who Are You Writing For?

What use is a film if no one wants to watch it, or a book if there are no readers to buy it? On the web, the surfers are your audience. They are the reason why you are writing.

So even before you start thinking of how to write the content for a website, ask that crucial question: Who am I writing for?

Then do everything you can to find out who these readers are, what do they like or dislike, how do they react and interact, what motivates and excites them, what sets them thinking...? Are they happy-go-surfing teenagers who want zany copy, cool links, lots of freebies, or older women looking for articles that are short and entertaining, or engineers looking for whitepapers and technical inputs?
Who is your target audience?

Target Audience

Imagine that a webzine has asked you to write an article on how to prepare Diwali sweets. Obviously, your readers will be people interested in knowing how to prepare the sweets. So what do you do? Take your mom's special recipes and consider your job done? Definitely not!

Categorically Speaking

Rule one of knowing your audience says: Don't generalise.

In this case, people interested in making Diwali sweets are the most obvious reader group. But when you put the three thousand-odd people who might read your article into one bracket, you are simply demolishing any guarantee that your planned content will match up against the needs of this vast audience.

Ideally, begin by breaking down your target audience into several different categories, even if it means that they are looking for just slightly different things from your site.

For example, your readers might include:

1. Experienced cooks
2. Inexperienced cooks
3. People from the same local region as you
4. People from other locations

Obviously, experienced cooks might come to your website looking for more fancy stuff than the rudimentary recipe that you put out. People with geographical diversity might have different expectations, especially if they are able to identify your website as belonging to a specific region, maybe they are looking for traditional recipes indigenous to your area or culture.

That should give you sufficient idea about how important it is to think of who are you writing for. Only when you are able to identify their needs will you be able to give them what they want, and keep them coming back for more!

Get Help

To find out who these readers are, you will need to do a bit of research. Your best resource will of course be your client. So don't hesitate about asking questions about the age, gender, academic background, work environment, needs, and expectations of the intended target audience. Then create a profile that defines the typical reader who will want to search and read your web content.

Knowing the audience profile makes your task definitely easier. For instance, if you identify that your audience consists of health-conscious or diabetic people looking for Diwali sweets made with low or no sugar content!

So that gives you an exact idea of the content required and narrows down the scope of your content.

Or, you might discover that the target audience belongs to a younger age group and does not necessarily know much about food beyond eating it! So that's another pointer on *how* you should write—the tone that you should use, the words that you should choose, the language syntax to be adopted, and above all, avoid complex instructions that might turn these first-time cooks away.

How Are You Going To Say It?

Longer, Deeper, Slower

Crafting attention-grabbing web content is not easy. As the writer, you will need to make sure that every element of your web page—from the headlines to the blurbs—is able to:

1. Hook the reader so that they continue beyond the headline.

2. Deliver a complete reading experience so that they bookmark your site or visit it again looking for more information.

3. Persuade them to hit the 'Next' button to read more and stay on your web pages for longer.

Make It Readable

If you don't want your website to languish in some unvisited corner of the web for time immemorial, make sure that your web content is readable, and compels the readers to come back for more. Here's how.

Repurpose, don't copy

Often, when a company hires you to write for their website, they will hand you their corporate literature as the source material for the web copy. It could include company brochures, product literatures, flyers, direct mailers, even annual reports. It is only natural to get swamped by the sheer volume of the text that's readily available to you. The temptation to use it all is great. After all, what are a few extra pages on the web? Besides, YOU are the one who is going to fashion all the navigation links.

Wait. Imagine that you have to attend a wedding reception this evening. You are trying to coordinate your jewellery—the diamond chandelier earrings, the fabulous gold choker, the gem-crusted bracelet.... You wouldn't be caught dead wearing all of them together, right? Your aim is to choose a piece that best suits your dress.

Similarly, when it comes to repurposing print material for your website, avoid going over the top. Your brief as a web writer is *not* to transfer the paper-based text into an html layout and link it all up with a 'Next' button. That's like committing copywriting hara-kiri.
Your job is to apply good web writing techniques to the paper-based text—brevity being the first one.

The problem of plenty

It is only natural for a writer to want to write and then write some more. I mean, our tribe loves words. Unfortunately, there's no guarantee that our readers can match our enthusiasm. So make sure that you edit those reams of paper to highlight the major ideas. Then rewrite to make them clear, concise and crisp.

The problem obviously is, knowing how much is too much. The ideal solution is to cut your content by half! You have got to shorten the existing text to less than 50% of its original size. Preserve meaning and do away with all the blah.

Keep It Simple and Short

The rule of KISS (that's the acronym for Keep It Simple, Stupid!) is VERY much applicable to web writing. Because once again, people don't read on the web. They scan.

So, after you have finished writing, honestly evaluate the content to see how many times would you have to re-read it before you can begin to make sense of it. Then ask yourself, if you were reading this content on the web, would you attempt to read it a second time? If the answer is no, rewrite your text. And this time make sure to you keep it simple, short and straightforward.

Before	After
The end of each week sees a meeting of the board of directors and lead analysts of each sector. The purpose of this meeting is to compile a combined report for informing the investors of the increased or decreased value of the XYZ Mutual Fund based on the market performance. It contains a summary of the major developments of the week plus includes information since the initial buy-in of equity. In these weekly reports, the XYZ Mutual Fund benchmarks its performance against the NSE Index.	The board of directors and lead analysts of the fund compile a weekly performance report for the investors. In addition to a summary of the previous weekly developments, the report also contains information about the performance since the fund started, using the NSE Index as a benchmark.

As it happens, and you must have discovered it, getting plain, simple words to flow out of your pen (or the keyboard) is an excruciatingly tough task. And it helps to steer clear of verbosity. Make sure that you:

1. Use short, crisp phrases
2. Use short words
3. Avoid long introductions to your text
4. Avoid convoluted syntax
5. Avoid jargon
6. Edit your text for redundancy. (For example, instead of saying 'in this day and age', you could simply use 'today')

Be concise

Although sometimes a wordsmith will plump up the text in response to the need for volume, and say the same thing in different ways, often wordiness in the text is because we struggle to find those right words to perfectly express our idea. As a result, the text is littered with empty phrases that are of little value to what you have to say. Worse, they build redundancy into your content, and words or phrases start getting repeated.

The obvious solution is to edit your document for brevity. A tough task for any writer, but not impossible.... After all, the aim is to trim the fat!

A good strategy is to put away your draft after you complete writing it. When you revisit it even a few hours later, you will find it easy to spot the superfluous words, meandering phrases, and empty ideas.
This is one of the most effective ways to improve your writing.

Before	After
For all intents and purposes, the agricultural productivity in India generally depends on certain factors that are really more to do with climate rather than the advances in the technological realm.	The agricultural productivity in India depends more on climatic conditions than technological advances.
We have gathered here for the purpose of deciding whether or not we should go ahead with the negotiations at this point in time.	We are here to decide if it is feasible to proceed with the negotiations now.
It is the opinion of his parents that he has failed to meet their expectations.	He has failed his parents' expectations.

Use active voice

We have heard this just so many times. But why use the active voice? What is wrong with saying "This book is written by me"? Nothing really.

But if I turn it around and say "I wrote this book", the focus immediately shifts from the doing word (the verb) to the doer (the subject). And that is what any written communication should aim to do. It should place the subject as the doer of all the action in a sentence.

On a web page, this can wonderfully energise your content.

Before	After
The ozone layer is being depleted because of the release of CFC gases into the environment.	The release of CFC gases is depleting the ozone layer.

Avoid jargon

Just type out the word jargon on your computer; select it; and press Shift+F7. Its synonyms will pop up, including—terminology and gobbledygook!

Confused? How can terminology also qualify as gobbledygook? Think of it this way: If you are familiar with the specialised, technical language or jargon of a trade, you will easily understand what's being said. So the jargon is terminology to you. But what if you are a newbie? You don't really understand the jargon. Naturally, it sounds like a lot of gobbledygook to you.

Moral of the story? If you don't want your content to sound like gibberish to your readers, AVOID jargon.

Before	After
Not all browsers support all standards laid out by the W3C.	Not all browsers support all standards laid out by the World Wide Web.

Write for an audience of one

Although the web is dubbed a mass medium, using a website is a very personal experience. That's because unlike television that you can watch with others, people view the web content from the comfort of their desktop or laptop. It's almost always one person per screen. What does that mean to you as a writer? Simply, that you need to write for *one* reader, not the entire market.

So, use a conversational tone. Write in the first and second person, using the pronouns 'I' and 'you'. That will help you *talk* to the reader, like you'd talk to a friend. You have succeeded if you can create a voice that mirrors who the reader is or better still, *wants* to be.

Some more tips:

1. Avoid starting your sentences with *there is/it is* or *there are*:

Before	After
It is difficult to drive in the thick winter fog.	Driving in the thick winter fog is difficult.

2. Avoid *which* or *that* or *who*. Instead, break up the sentence.

Before	After
The book which I was reading is not very interesting.	I read the book. It's not very interesting.

3. Avoid nouns formed from verbs. E.g., words ending in '–tion' or '–sion'. Instead, use the verb.

Before	After
He submitted an application for the job.	He applied for the job.

Edit, edit, edit – Quick recap

Good writing is really about removing words, because it is harder to create a short sentence than a long, rambling one with the same meaning. That makes editing a *very* important final task in the writing process. It involves polishing your content by improving the grammar, punctuation, and consistency, and by making content suggestions.

1. Get to the point and remove everything else. Remember, people don't read on the web, they only scan! So, don't bury important information in a block of text, or at the end of a long page.

2. Write for an audience of one. Use conversational tone and speak in the first and second person.

3. Avoid jargon and acronyms, unless you know that every reader will understand.

4. Think short. Short words. Short sentences. Short paragraphs.

5. Use bullet points or bold type to help important points stand out.

6. Never underline for emphasis. On a web page, underlining means a link.

Linked-In

When you shorten the text, your first concern is whether the information is important enough to be included. But what happens when the information is not useful for a casual reader, but would definitely interest a visitor looking for substantiated data?

For example, you are writing for a website on climate change and its effects. You need to include a huge statistical data to substantiate the claims in your article. But you are afraid that it might turn off the first-time reader who wants to know about how his frequent flying is adding to global warming. At the same time, your target audience also includes serious researchers who will quote your website in their thesis only if they get proof to back up what they are saying.

The solution? Link it. Put the additional information on another page and provide a hyperlink which the reader can follow if they wish to. You could even save the information as a .pdf file and leave the link at the appropriate point on the web page. So if a reader wants to view it, they can do so by opening the .pdf file, instead of scrolling through pages of content.
This will also make it easier for the reader to download the report and save it on their computer, or even print it to read later.

Before	After
Click here to see the report.	Review our year to date performance. (.pdf 210 kb)

Pictures are worth a thousand words

This really does not need any explanation. We all know of situations that are better depicted by a single picture than text. For instance, a news website report talking about the severity of an accident, a real estate website giving the description of a country house with a walled garden, a fashion designer's website with the release of latest haute couture lines. In all these situations, and in many others, pictures can be a crucial aid in grabbing eyeballs.

Apart from providing photographic evidence, we can exploit the visual nature of the Internet to quickly and effectively represent tabular data. For example, using tables, charts, or graphs for numerical data is a great way to categorise and display information. It not only reduces the lines of your text, you are also able to display vital data in a manner that's easy and quick to understand.

Note: Tables are an effective tool when it comes to visualising data or displaying tabular data that needs to be compared. They are also an important element for good layout and design.

<table>
<tr><th>Before</th><th colspan="2">After</th></tr>
<tr><td rowspan="5">All India e-Learning Association

ID Consortium (2/08/07) (Word Document): Summarised minutes from the meeting prepared by AK Sharma.
(same document in pdf format)

ID Consortium (8/10/07) (Word document): Summarised minutes from the meeting prepared by AK Sharma.

ID Consortium (12/12/07) (Word document): Summarised minutes from the meeting prepared by AK Sharma.</td><td colspan="2">All Indian e-Learning Association Meeting Minutes

All .pdf documents require Adobe Acrobat.</td></tr>
<tr><td>Meeting Date</td><td>Meeting Title</td></tr>
<tr><td>2/08/07</td><td>Trends in Web-based Learning
(.pdf 59kb)</td></tr>
<tr><td>8/10/07</td><td>Executive Education Best Practices
(.pdf 87 kb)</td></tr>
<tr><td>12/12/07</td><td>e-Learning and the Literacy Drive
(.pdf 36 kb)</td></tr>
</table>

Make It Scannable

Chunk de!

"Chunking" means dividing information into small, clear pieces or chunks. Perhaps the most complex part of the web writing process, this is the litmus test for your analytical skills. It needs you to decide which information is important, what information to present, and how to organise it.

Chunking is crucial to getting your visitors to read the content because it allows them to scan ten short "chunks" of information that are interlinked, instead of making them scroll through a seemingly endless web page.

When you organise your content as one long block of text, you place all major concepts onto a single page, with little scope to highlight them. When a reader skims through the long page, it is not only difficult to locate the information they are searching, it is quite likely that they will miss it.

www.bplans.com

Notice the links on the left for easy navigation to any part of the business plan. Also note that the introduction to the Executive Summary is placed on this page, along with the option of navigating to the next page of the same section.

Instead, organising your content into small, scannable chunks makes it easier to 'see' if a page contains the relevant information. Readers are also motivated to 'check out' the next few pages when they see that they can quickly scan a page.

For example, an entrepreneur wants to write a business plan for his new venture. He needs information about how to write the market analysis. He uses the keywords 'How to write a business plan' to run a search on the Internet. He reaches a website that gives him details about how to write the Executive Summary of a business plan. He likes the way the information is presented, and decides to follow the links placed in the left menu to see if the market analysis page is just as relevant.

As you can see, chunking works well with the hyperlinked, hierarchical structure of websites, since most websites are organised to present the home page first, offering a general overview of the site, and progress down through increasingly specific submenus and content pages. More importantly, creating web pages with relevant headlines and chunked information increases the probability of your content being listed higher by a search engine.

When you place your chunks in this hierarchical structure, aim for one main idea per page. So if you have a long article, put one central idea and its supporting arguments as one chunk on one page.
At the same time, remember that your readers won't click from page to page to read different sub-sections of an article.

Here is another example of a corporate home page with links to different content pages and menus. Notice how it chunks information by incorporating links to background material in the .pdf format.
This is an excellent strategy for making in-depth material available to serious visitors but keeping it away from a casual reader who might move away if the page is too slow to load.

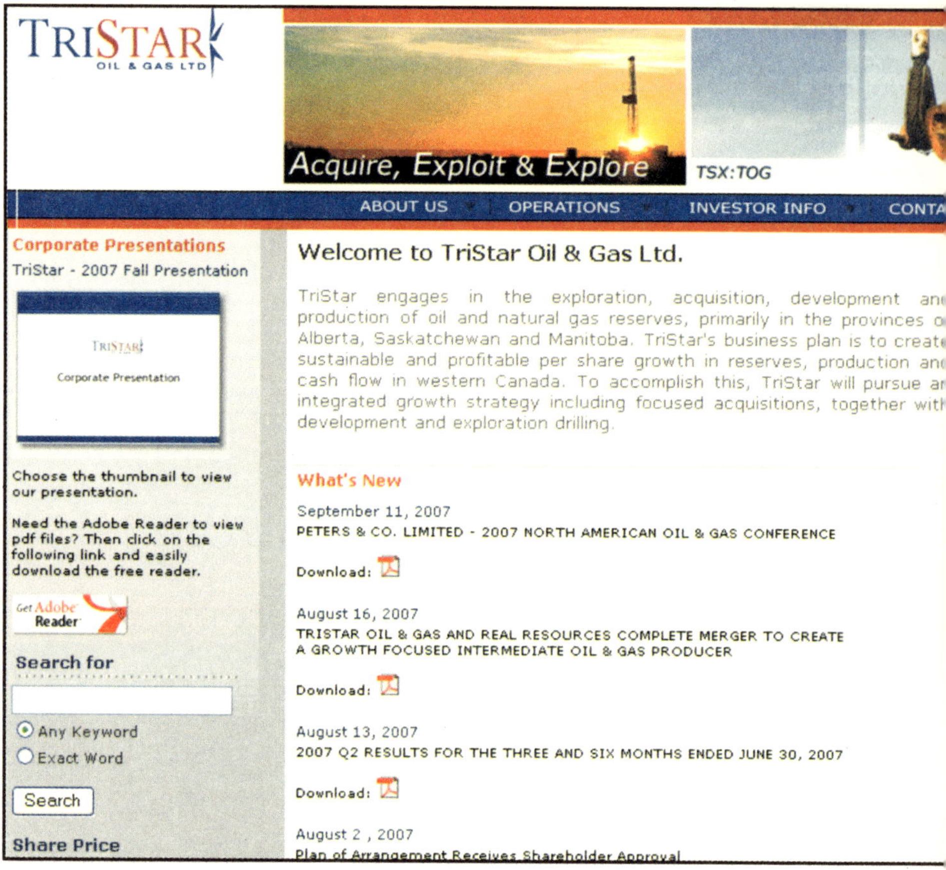

www.tristar.com

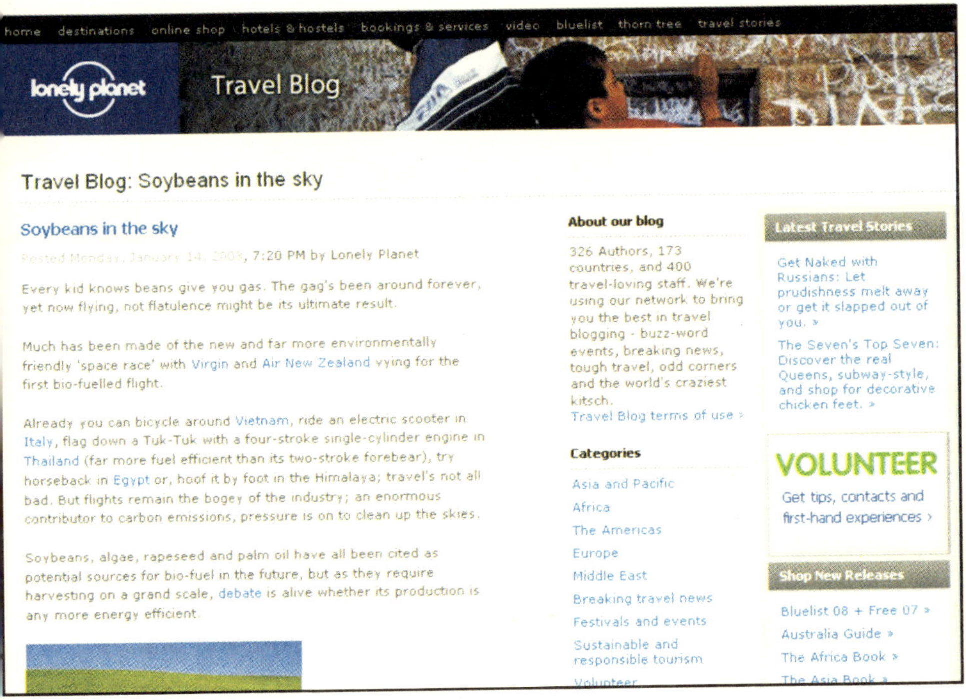

home destinations online shop hotels & hostels bookings & services video bluelist thorn tree travel stories

lonely planet Travel Blog

Travel Blog: Soybeans in the sky

Soybeans in the sky

Posted Monday, January 14, 2008, 7:20 PM by Lonely Planet

Every kid knows beans give you gas. The gag's been around forever, yet now flying, not flatulence might be its ultimate result.

Much has been made of the new and far more environmentally friendly 'space race' with Virgin and Air New Zealand vying for the first bio-fuelled flight.

Already you can bicycle around Vietnam, ride an electric scooter in Italy, flag down a Tuk-Tuk with a four-stroke single-cylinder engine in Thailand (far more fuel efficient than its two-stroke forebear), try horseback in Egypt or, hoof it by foot in the Himalaya; travel's not all bad. But flights remain the bogey of the industry; an enormous contributor to carbon emissions, pressure is on to clean up the skies.

Soybeans, algae, rapeseed and palm oil have all been cited as potential sources for bio-fuel in the future, but as they require harvesting on a grand scale, debate is alive whether its production is any more energy efficient.

About our blog

326 Authors, 173 countries, and 400 travel-loving staff. We're using our network to bring you the best in travel blogging - buzz-word events, breaking news, tough travel, odd corners and the world's craziest kitsch.
Travel Blog terms of use ›

Categories

Asia and Pacific
Africa
The Americas
Europe
Middle East
Breaking travel news
Festivals and events
Sustainable and responsible tourism
Volunteer

Latest Travel Stories

Get Naked with Russians: Let prudishness melt away or get it slapped out of you. »

The Seven's Top Seven: Discover the real Queens, subway-style, and shop for decorative chicken feet. »

VOLUNTEER
Get tips, contacts and first-hand experiences ›

Shop New Releases

Bluelist 08 + Free 07 »
Australia Guide »
The Africa Book »
The Asia Book »

www.lonelyplanet.com

The inverted pyramid

Schools—where we learn to write—traditionally teach us to use the pyramid style. Here, we work our way backwards—starting with general view and ending with the conclusion. For example, in response to a question that asks why the Rising of 1857 failed, students start with giving background information about the mutiny and its participants before listing the reasons for its failure.

Now imagine that you are a war journalist, covering the Rising. How would you report it? You would start with the most important part of your news—the conclusion—"The Rising Quelled". This will be followed by the subheading "Mangal Pandey to be hanged". The opening paragraph of the news will read something like "Following Laxmibai's death in a fierce battle, the leaders of the Rising have either been captured or forced to flee into exile...." Once you have caught the reader's interest, you will explore the reasons behind this in greater detail.

This is the journalistic or the inverted pyramid style of writing. Here, you start with the conclusion and then work down to greater levels of detail.

This approach works well on the web. And it's not difficult to guess why. Primarily because by stating the most important first, you proactively grab the audience attention. And when the readers get an interesting piece of information, they want to know why it happened or how it works, or where was it effected. Also, gradual progression into in-depth details facilitates further scanning, and also enables the readers to stop at any level of detail that suits their interest.

Africa
Americas
Asia-Pacific
Europe
Middle East
South Asia
UK
Business
Health
cience/Nature
Technology
Entertainment
lso in the news

Video and Audio

Have Your Say
In Pictures
Country Profiles
Special Reports

ATED BBC SITES
SPORT
WEATHER
ON THIS DAY
EDITORS' BLOG

LANGUAGES
اردو
हिन्दी
বাংলা
پښتو
नेपाली
தமிழ்
සිංහල
MORE >

New term for civilian Musharraf

Pakistani President Pervez Musharraf has been sworn in for a second term, this time as a civilian ruler, calling it a "historic day" for the country.

Mr Musharraf called for "political reconciliation" and insisted polls for parliament would go ahead in January.

Mr Musharraf promised elections would be held in January

OPEN Enlarge Image

As he was being sworn in, about 200 lawyers opposed to his rule clashed violently with police in Lahore.

On Wednesday, Mr Musharraf stepped down as commander of the military amid heavy domestic and international pressure.

Correspondents say there will be more stiff challenges to his leadership in the weeks ahead, following his imposition of emergency rule on 3 November.

'Protect and defend'

Pervez Musharraf won a second term as president in a legislative election on 6 October, the legitimacy of which has been hotly contested.

For Thursday's ceremony, the president arrived in a black traditional suit (sherwani) instead of a military uniform.

The ceremony began with the playing of Pakistan's national anthem and a recitation from the Koran.

"We understand our society, our environment, better than anyone in the West"

President Musharraf

Musharraf's message to army

He read out an oath to "preserve, protect and defend

VIDEO AND AUDIO NEWS
President Musharraf's swearing in ceremony
WATCH

PAKISTAN'S POLITICAL CRISIS
LATEST NEWS
- Musharraf gives up army uniform
- Pakistan rivals enter poll fray
- Sharif welcomed back to Lahore
- Pakistan troops in Swat offensive

ANALYSIS AND BACKGROUND
Change of heart
Why Gen Musharraf has allowed Nawaz Sharif home
- Options open for Musharraf
- US policy in the balance
- Q&A: Political crisis
- Your questions: Emergency rule
- Timeline: Political rivals
- How the 1999 coup unfolded
- Pakistan's circular history

PROFILES
Pervez Musharraf Go

TROUBLED BORDER REGION
- Pakistan's Taleban's backyard
- Army's tribal quagmire

AUDIO AND VIDEO
WATCH Path to emergency

YOUR SAY
- Military handover

RELATED INTERNET LINKS
- Pakistani government
- Pakistan People's Party
- PML-N

The BBC is not responsible for the content of external internet sites

www.bbc.com

This news story is a classic example of the inverted pyramid. It starts with a synopsis of the news item, followed by the main points.

Then it launches a more detailed description of events, again with a comment in bold typeface. Also, note the blue link in the right bottom corner that will take you to related chunked content placed elsewhere in the website.

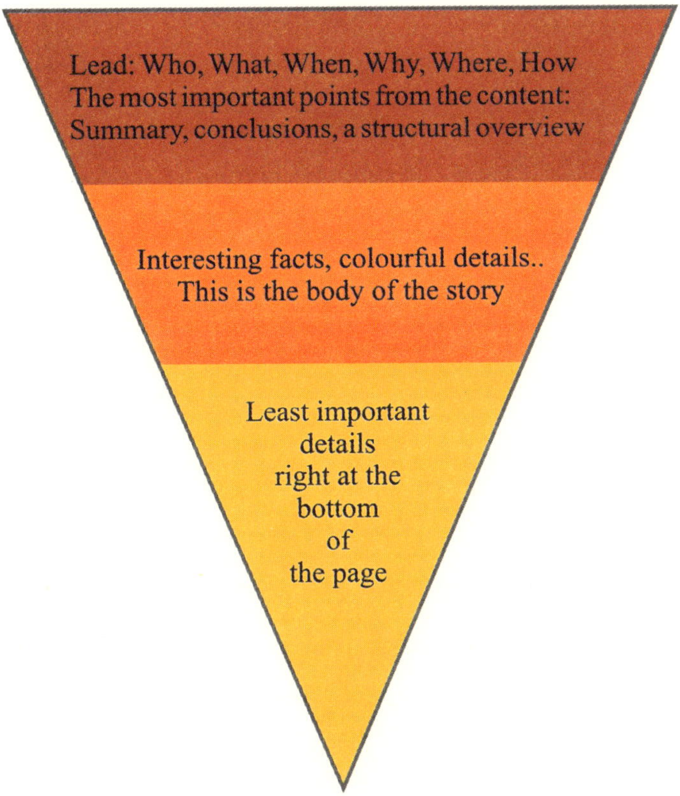

The inverted pyramid style is great for presenting web content because when people read online they tend to scan quickly, looking for key points. Even when they do slow down to read web pages, they often stop reading before the end. The idea behind the inverted pyramid writing style is that you should start with the most important information first, and then put the less important information at the bottom, so that even if the reader moves away, they have registered the most important piece of information before they leave.

To understand this better, just picture an upside down triangle, with the wide end at the top of the page and the pointy end at the bottom. That's how your writing will flow, with the most important information at the very top of the content.

Here's a quick checklist for you to know that you have got your inverted pyramid right.

1. **Most important things first:** This will help readers to decide just how relevant your article is in their search for information.

2. **Get to the point:** Don't expect the reader to ferret out the most important information from your article.

3. **Your reader is scanning your copy:** Bold headings, bulleted lists, and clever catch-phrases as hyperlinks are ways to help readers scan your article. It helps them pick and choose the information they need.

Reduce scrolling

What's your experience with long scrolling pages? According to Jakob Nielsen, the Usability Guru, users will almost never scroll through very long pages. That's because very long web pages tend to be disorienting, as they require the reader to scroll long distances and remember the organisation of content that he has scrolled through. So what's the solution?

As we saw before, chunking is the solution. Just break up the piece into a series of shorter chunks, and link them together. If you have a page that people will want to read at length, provide a printer-friendly version. This is helpful because the reader can print or save the entire document at once and avoid scrolling the screen or jumping between pages.

Headings are important

Headline is the one-line summary of your content on top of your web page. As you saw in the inverted pyramid, the most important part of your content area is the top of the page. That's the only area you can be sure your users will see without having to scroll. Use it to your advantage. Put a headline where the reader can immediately know whether the subject of any given page interests him.

Now let's see some of the ways to craft an attention-grabbing headline that will hold your reader's attention and keep them reading.

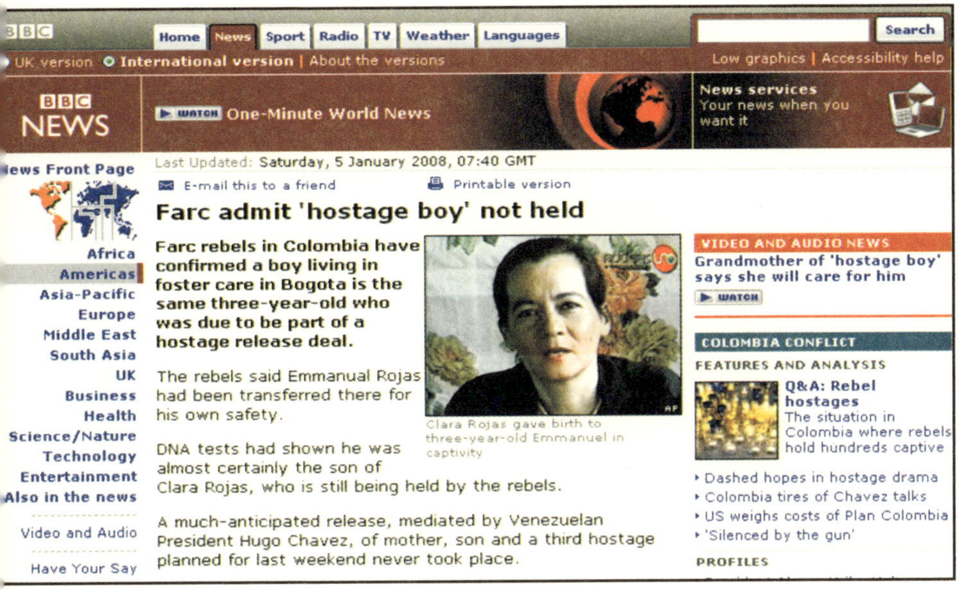

BBC | Home | News | Sport | Radio | TV | Weather | Languages | Search

UK version · International version | About the versions · Low graphics | Accessibility help

BBC NEWS · WATCH One-Minute World News · News services Your news when you want it

News Front Page · Africa · Americas · Asia-Pacific · Europe · Middle East · South Asia · UK · Business · Health · Science/Nature · Technology · Entertainment · Also in the news · Video and Audio · Have Your Say

Last Updated: Saturday, 5 January 2008, 07:40 GMT

E-mail this to a friend · Printable version

Farc admit 'hostage boy' not held

Farc rebels in Colombia have confirmed a boy living in foster care in Bogota is the same three-year-old who was due to be part of a hostage release deal.

The rebels said Emmanual Rojas had been transferred there for his own safety.

DNA tests had shown he was almost certainly the son of Clara Rojas, who is still being held by the rebels.

A much-anticipated release, mediated by Venezuelan President Hugo Chavez, of mother, son and a third hostage planned for last weekend never took place.

Clara Rojas gave birth to three-year-old Emmanuel in captivity

VIDEO AND AUDIO NEWS

Grandmother of 'hostage boy' says she will care for him · WATCH

COLOMBIA CONFLICT

FEATURES AND ANALYSIS

Q&A: Rebel hostages — The situation in Colombia where rebels hold hundreds captive

- Dashed hopes in hostage drama
- Colombia tires of Chavez talks
- US weighs costs of Plan Colombia
- 'Silenced by the gun'

PROFILES

BBC | Home | News | Sport | Radio | TV | Weather | Languages

UK version · International version | About the versions · Low graphics | A

BBC NEWS · WATCH One-Minute World News · News services Your news when y want it

News Front Page · Africa · Americas · Asia-Pacific · Europe · Middle East · South Asia · UK · Business · Health · Science/Nature · Technology

Last Updated: Friday, 4 January 2008, 09:30 GMT

E-mail this to a friend · Printable version

UK detectives arrive in Pakistan

A team of Scotland Yard investigators has arrived in Pakistan to assist in the inquiry into the assassination of former Prime Minister Benazir Bhutto.

Earlier, President Pervez Musharraf said he was "not fully satisfied" with the investigation into the killing.

Scotland Yard and Pakistan

VIDEO AND AUDI

The UK detective Pakistan · WATCH

PAKISTAN'S POLIT

BENAZIR BHUTTO A

Electi Who be election Februa

- Bhutto obituary

What grabs their attention

Here are four easy ways to write headlines that grab the reader's attention:

1. **Fan their desires:** When it comes to our wish lists, we are all human—religion, race, gender no bar! Read the sample headlines below and see if they wouldn't make you want to know how to make your desires come true.

    a. Make more money and pay less tax!

    b. Look 10 years younger in 10 days!

    c. Lose the weight you hate!

    d. Find real love and genuine happiness!

    e. Be successful, up your status!

    f. Eat, drink and be healthy!

    g. Chill... get more time off!

2. **Recognise their fears:** People across the globe also have pretty much the same fears. We all want to know how to:

    a. Avoid making costly mistakes

    b. Not lose out on an opportunity

    c. Keep safe

3. **Touch their emotions:** Again a universal pattern emerges here.

    a. Why we all hate our boss!

    b. No more Monday morning blues!

    c. Throw away your glasses forever!

4. **Arouse their curiosity:** And again, the common factor...call it interest, nosiness, prying, snooping, or inquisitiveness...we all want to know how.

    a. How 'xyz' turned a simple idea into a million dollars.

b. Double your income overnight with this one simple strategy.

c. What New Year resolutions did Britney make this year?

How to write headlines

Next, we move on to how to actually *craft* those attention-grabbing headlines. Headlines, as you know by now, are a writer's biggest chance to compel the reader to read more. What you don't know is that you have less than five seconds to do it!

The Testimonial Headline

Testimonials make very powerful headlines. That's because they are a proof that someone else has found your product or service to offer the value that it promises. Testimonials use the actual views of your existing customers to vouch for the truth in your offer.

For example, the wealth creation services of a bank can have a satisfied customer say:

"I saved...now I earn $ssss and have financial freedom!"

The News Headline

Typically, news headlines aim to get the reader involved and make him feel part of your venture from the very beginning. They are especially effective when you want to make a product launch or announce an improved version.

For example, you are writing an update on a company website about the release of an upgraded software version:

"Introducing iBook 3.2"

The How To Headline

The 'how to' headline promises a winning formula. It suggests that the solution will be revealed in the article, and compels the user to read on.

For example:

"How to lose 5 kilos in 1 week...with just 5 minutes a day"!

The Question Headline

Ever heard of leading questions? It means asking questions in a way that will elicit the response you are looking for. For example, "Would you like to go on an all expense-paid cruise?" I don't know many people who wouldn't answer 'yes' to that!

The advantage of using question headlines is that you are setting the tone and expectation for the article that will follow. Plus, you have already created a positive expectation in the reader's mind. Just be sure to answer the 'how' in your article!

Command Headline

This type of headline creates a sense of urgency in the reader's mind. Use words that command attention and urge the reader into a desired action.

It could be as simple as a blurb at the end of an interesting article saying, "Subscribe to xyz newsletter today!" On the other hand, it could play on the reader's desires and say:

"Act now and save £1000 on your insurance
this year!"

Hype Headline

Go into the superlative! Build a headline that boosts your product image.

For example, which of the two headlines below would you choose for an email subscription offer for a job portal?

1. Subscribe to get that coveted job!

OR

2. The easiest way to land the best job!

It has to be the second headline. It gets the reader to know what makes your service deliver not just a job, but the *best* job in the *easiest* way.

Reason Why Headline

This is a great way to help the readers focus on the features of your product. For example, "Linux over Windows: 10 top features".

If your product is as well known, you need not even say "10 top features why you should choose Linux over Windows."

Some more tips:

Use subheadings

Subheadings help to keep up the reader's interest levels, and focus his attention as they talk about the most compelling benefit of your product. You can use several subheadings throughout the body copy.

Use bulleted or numbered lists

Numbered as well as bulleted lists make sense because they will help you draw attention to important information. For readers too, lists are visually appealing and make it easy to quickly find pertinent information.

Here's an example of a travel guide detailing how to avoid jet lag. Decide which one offered you the most readability:

Before	After
Flying internationally causes jetlag because of the fact that you are crossing three time zones. Make sure that you drink plenty of water and avoid consuming alcohol on-board. It's best to stick with a bland diet. If you are travelling to a different time zone, adjust your watch according to your destination's time clock and attempt to adhere to your arrival schedule. Also, it would be a good idea to take some sleeping pills on a long flight over, so you can catch up on your sleep during the flight.	**AVOID JETLAG** Flying internationally causes jetlag because of the fact that you are crossing time zones. Some precautions to take include: a) drinking plenty of water. b) avoiding alcohol intake. c) sticking with a bland diet. d) adjusting your watch according to your destination's time clock and attempt to adhere to your arrival schedule. e) taking some sleeping pills on that long flight over; you'll be thankful for it when you arrive.

Those Cool, Blue Links

Make links accessible

Hyperlinks are fun. They allow us to navigate our way through the virtual space. They give us the freedom to go wherever and read whatever. They give websites their non-linear structure, and allow us to jump forward, backward or away from pages. In fact, if there were no hyperlinks, there wouldn't be too much to look forward to on the web. Naturally, they are an important part of writing on the web.

As part of a high-level design, hyperlinks connect different segments of a website, and that makes them crucial to creating the site map. At a more micro-level, they also link the different chunks of an information block.

Many writers feel that hyperlinks within a document will cause the reader to lose the thread of discussion. Worse, they fear that hyperlinks will take them away from the web page, and try to enforce a linear path of navigation by placing the 'Next' buttons at the bottom of the chunk.

Bad strategy! Because if users don't like what they are reading, they always have the option of hitting the 'Back' button of the browser and moving away.

Instead, get smart and embed many links within the text and allow them to explore the information that you have to offer. They are bound to find something interesting and stay on your website longer than they intended. See example on page no. 55.

http://www.createlinks.com/cps/rde/xchg/au_division_web_link/hs.xsl/blue_text.htm

We all know that there's a programming language at work behind those web pages. But your readers are not here to read the code; they prefer stuff that humans can read. Providing links that read like a string of alphabets in random order or even links telling them to "click here for more information" or "click here to send email" are neither very informative nor motivating enough to act as you want them to. Instead, they might just wander away from your site.

A better idea that will work in your interest is to indicate what they can expect to find when they click on a link. If the blue, underlined text is an interesting word or phrase, there are more chances that they will click to know more. For example, "If you are going white-water rafting these holidays, here are some adventurous places you might want to consider."

It's okay to offer different links that lead to the same page. In all likelihood, the users will not return to a previous page to explore the other links because they will find some more links of interest on the page that they have reached. But by placing multiple routes to the same information you have increased the possibility of your content being read.

Besides navigation, hyperlinks also allow you to place downloadable objects on your page. The only care that you should take is to give a description of that object. For example, state the type of file they are downloading and its size.

Write To Be Found

The World Wide Web is a rich repository of information that you, as web writers, create. People search for this information by typing in keywords or phrases into Search Engines. That makes Search Engines an important tool for you to reach your intended target audience.

But what makes a Search Engine list one website before the other? Is there any logic to it?

Sure, there is!

Search Engine Optimisation

Very few of your visitors will ever reach your website by physically typing in the URL. Most will have followed a link found by search engines. That makes it *very, very* important to ensure that your web pages are *seen* by search engines. There are ways to improve your website's chances of being found via search engines. But before that let's just quickly understand how search engines work.

Types of engines

There are two types of search engines:

1. Spider/Crawler-based: For example, Google. Spider-based engines have three parts:

    a. crawler

    b. index

    c. software for ranking

2. Human Powered: Static lists of websites

Crawling

A search engine uses software called a "web spider" or "web crawler", which is a type of "bot" (short for "robot") used to automatically carry out repetitive tasks.

The spider browses the World Wide Web, starting with heavily used sites. It "crawls" from site to site, following links and "reading" the content displayed there.

Indexing

The spider builds a list of web pages and words. The search engine then creates a database of these words called an index. When you type in a word or phrase for search, the engine compares your keyword or phrase to its index and compiles a list of links to pages that match your enquiry. This is what you see as your search results.

Ranking

Search engines use sophisticated algorithms for ranking their results. If you have noticed, the ranking can differ for different search engines. That is because they differ slightly in how they compile and index their data, but for every indexed web page, these search engines analyse data about specific internal and external factors.

Internal factors include keywords, page descriptions and page titles which are written within the source html code. External factors include links from other sites. The idea is that other sites will link to a web page if it contains helpful, relevant information.
The more links into a page from other sites, the higher ranking it deserves.

Tips for good search engine rankings:

1. Write content helpful and useful. The better your content, the more other sites will link to it; and the more they link to your site, the more the recognition from search engines.
2. Write one main topic or subject per page. This allows clearer matches with searches.
3. Craft a headline that uses the main idea of each page. Then, talk about it in the first paragraph. Search engines give more weight to words at the beginning of a page.
4. When you write the content, try and use words and phrases that users are most likely to use when searching for relevant information. Avoid jargon and focus on adopting your customers' lingo.
5. Search engines may not be able to detect text placed inside Flash animations.
6. Include ALT text for the images on your pages. These tags should be words that give out information about your content. For example, if you are writing about Flower Remedies, use the

names of the flowers or the remedies as ALT text, such as Cherry Plum or Star of Bethlehem instead of flower1, flower2, etc. This is because search engines read ALT text like other text on your site. So when a user is looking for information on a specific flower remedy, your page will be listed higher if the images have relevant ALT tags.

7. Another secret to building websites that show up higher in search engine ranks is using descriptive page titles, page descriptions and keywords, or metadata.

Develop A Style Guide

Is it web site or website... should the full stop come before the quote or after the quote... what kind of bullet lists should we use.... These and many more questions are resolved when you put a style guide in place before starting work on the web content.

Style guides help in making your web text consistent in terms of spellings, grammar usage, and presentation. Plus, they make it easy for you to coordinate and seamlessly integrate the works of different writers if you are working with a large team on an ongoing project.

Write Right

Style guides are the standards for design and writing. Standards for writing define such specifications as punctuation, grammar, spellings, etc. This helps when working with a team of writers and editors, since guidelines for linguistic correctness are built into the content from the word go. It removes any doubts one might have about language and grammar technicalities, as well as a particular style of writing a word.
For example, it helps you establish at the outset if e-mail should be hyphenated, or the word Web should be capitalised.

Once the style guide is in place, every content writer in the team must treat it as the Bible of everything 'language'. For that reason, make sure that you make it as exhaustive as possible, including not only the terminology and usage specific to your topic or industry, but also the styles for:

1. Writing numbers. For example, should you write numbers as numerals or should you spell them out,

or what format should you use when writing dates, or time, or monetary figures, or measurements? The style guide tells you how.

2. Spelling and usage of technical and Internet terminology. For example, is it E-learning, e-learning, e-Learning?

Note: The thumb rule when creating guidelines for brand names or company names is to adopt your client's style. For example, you cannot correct the name "Dreamz Unlimited" to "Dreams Unlimited" because your spellchecker says so. Spellings of company names and products are outside the authority of a style guide!

A major benefit of having a style guide is that it ensures consistency. It not only helps make your documents grammatically error-proof, but also helps your readers to identify titles, headlines, and subheadings in your documents while navigating. In the images given on page no. 63, notice the headline style (sentence case), subheadings (or lack of them), etc. give an immediate feel of identity to the web pages, although these screenshots belong to different sections of the website.

Layout Right

Let's recognise it—writers are basically text people. And designing a website is a job best left to the designers. But sometimes it is possible that we are forced to double up as designers, especially when putting up an individual web page or if you are a small business owner working on a tight budget.

While this guide is exclusively for web writers, here are a few basic style tips for visual design and layout of web pages for easier reading:

1. Use white space. Remember that reading on the computer screen is different from a paper document. Tightly spaced text on a computer screen is hard on the eyes. So ensure that you use a layout that allows enough white space around the text.

Tip: An easy way to do this is to enlarge the margins or narrow the width of text lines.

2. Use short paragraphs, bullets, numbered lists and tables in your layout. This will help the users to quickly locate the information they are seeking.

3. Make the important text bold to highlight it.

Tip: Avoid underlining words because on the web underlined words are hyperlinks.

4. Use colour to draw attention to important headings, subheadings or keywords. If you are having trouble figuring out a colour palette for your website, try to harmonise the shades with other elements such as your logo to create colour harmony.

Tip: Blue denotes hyperlinks. So avoid it while highlighting text.

5. Place your text on a contrasting background. Using black on white is a good practice that is also easy on the readers' eyes.

6. Sans serif fonts make it easy to read on computer screens. Font size 10 is the standard for readability.

7. Avoid using animations, especially the loop animations, as they divert the viewer's attention away from the website's content with their continuous motion.

8. If you use images, make sure that they are small in size and easy to load. Users will invariably click away if they have to wait for different elements of a web page (videos, animations, images, sound, etc.) to load before they can see the content in its entirety.

9. Sometimes, it a good idea to give a download link if you want the reader to be able to access certain data from the relevant page. For instance, it's a good idea to provide a .pdf link for a business plan template on a page that explains the different elements of an effective business plan. But don't go overboard with the download feature. A website with several download links can get annoying.

Glossary

Address Bar	This is where we type the address (URL) of the website or web page that we want to access.
Affiliate Programs	Commission-based programs aimed at driving targeted traffic to a site. Typically, the referring site is paid on purchases made by the visitors who follow the link put up on your website/ web page.
ALT Text	Description that pops up in a text box when you put the cursor over the image.
Blog	An online Journal.
FAQs	A commonly used abbreviation for "frequently asked questions".
Firewall	A system that shields a private network (Intranet) from access by unauthorised users.
Intranet	An Intranet is a private network contained within an organisation that uses computers.

Pixels	Short for Picture Element; a single point in a graphic image.
Search Engines	Programs such as Yahoo, Altavista, HotBot, Excite, and Google that help users to locate the information on the web.
Style Guide	A document that contains the specifications of writing style such as punctuation, spelling, capitalisation, and language usage for consistency of text.
URL	Uniform Resource Locator, or web address
Web Page	A document generally formatted in HTML and containing content such as text, graphic images, and multimedia effects (sound files, video and/or animation files), plus other programming elements such as Java and JavaScript.
Website	A collection of web pages
Webzine	Web-based magazine
World Wide Web	The World Wide Web is the network of web pages on the Internet which can be viewed using browser software.